-WORKBOOK- for TEENS

Mindful Moments

Being Yourself is One of the Most Powerful Elements of Great Health

03

About Me

My name is

My big dreams

I like   I don't like

What Do I Think About Me

My favorite :

Food
Drink
Color
Animals

Describe me in 3 words

Table of Content

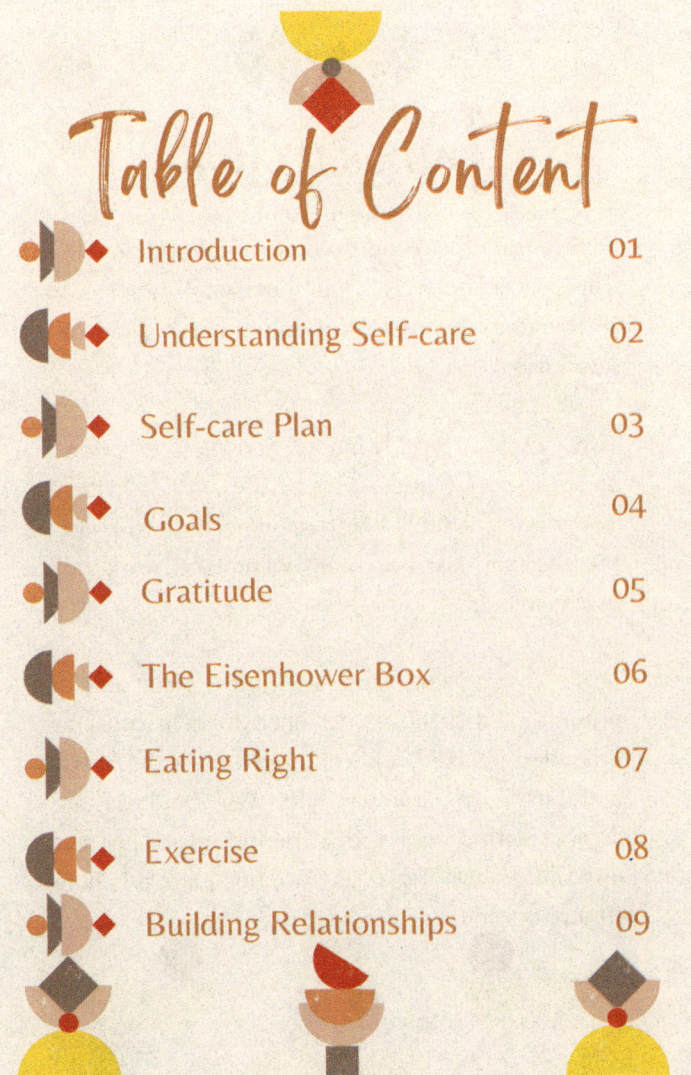

- Introduction — 01
- Understanding Self-care — 02
- Self-care Plan — 03
- Goals — 04
- Gratitude — 05
- The Eisenhower Box — 06
- Eating Right — 07
- Exercise — 08
- Building Relationships — 09

Introduction

Welcome to the Mindful Moments Workbook! This workbook is your personal guide to discovering the power of mindfulness and self-awareness.

Life can be a whirlwind of activities, emotions, and responsibilities, especially as a teen. Sometimes, it feels like there's no time to pause, breathe, and just be. That's where this workbook comes in.

Inside these pages, you will find a collection of prompts and practices designed to help you stay grounded, relaxed, and centered amidst the hustle and bustle of everyday life. Whether you are dealing with school stress, friendships, or just the ups and downs of growing up, this journal is here to support you.

Understanding Self-care

02

Self-care is all about taking time to care for your mind, body, spirit and emotions. It iss not just about pampering yourself, but about making choices that help you stay healthy, happy, and balanced.

As a teen, you have a lot going on, from school and extracurricular activities to friendships and family responsibilities. It is important to remember that taking care of yourself is just as important as taking care of your responsibilities.

Self-care means different things to different people, but at its core, it is about recognizing your needs and making time to meet them. It is about listening to your body and mind, understanding what they need, and taking steps to fulfill those needs.

Self-care is not a one-time activity; it is a regular practice that helps you maintain your well-being.

My Own Definition of Self Care

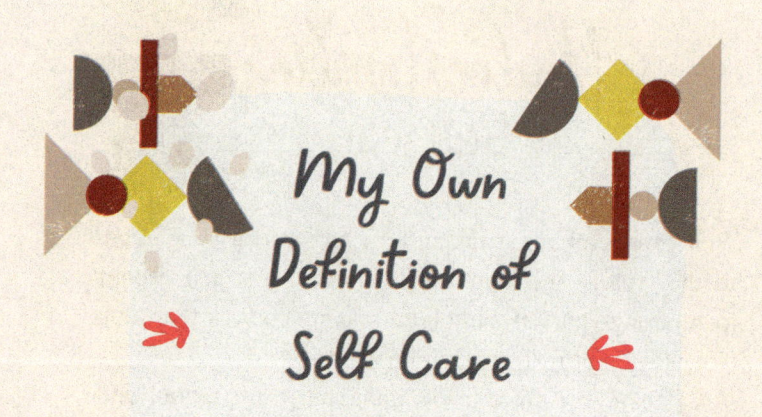

What makes YOU feel good? Take steps to incorporate those activities into your daily life. Self-care is personal, and it is all about finding what works best for YOU.

How Do I Take Care Of Myself?

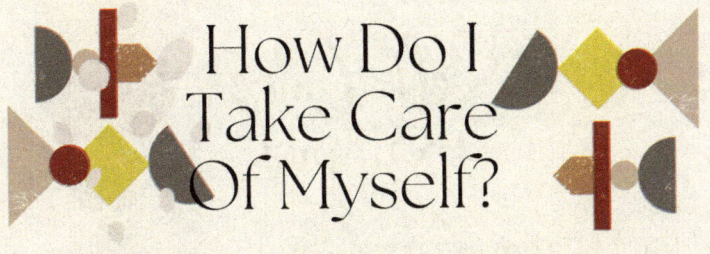

Self Care Examples

02

Listening to Music:
Create a playlist of your favourite songs and take some time to chill and enjoy the music.

Journaling:
Write down your thoughts, feelings, and experiences in a journal. It's a great way to process emotions and clear your mind.

Physical Activity:
Go for a walk, join a sports team, or try a new workout routine. Moving your body can boost your mood and energy levels.

Spending Time with Friends:
Hang out with friends who make you feel good. Plan a fun activity, have a movie night, or just chat and laugh together.

Self Care Examples

02

Reading:
Find a book you enjoy and get lost in the story. Reading can be a great adventure and a way to relax.

Taking a Break from Social Media:
Give yourself a break from social media for a day or a few hours. Use the time to focus on yourself and your offline activities.

Trying a New Hobby:
Explore a new hobby or activity that interests you, like painting, cooking, or playing an instrument.

Practicing Mindfulness or Meditation:
Spend a few minutes each day practicing mindfulness or meditation. It can help you stay present and reduce stress & anxiety.

Self Care Examples

02

Getting Enough Sleep:
Make sure you are getting enough rest. Establish a bedtime routine and aim for 8-10 hours of sleep each night.

Eating Nutritious Foods:
Fuel your body with healthy foods that make you feel good. Try incorporating more fruits, vegetables, and whole grains into your diet.

Taking Care of Your Skin:
Develop a skincare routine that works for you. Washing your face and moisturizing can be a simple way to feel refreshed.

Spending Time in Nature:
Get outside and enjoy nature. Go for a hike, visit a park, or simply sit outside and breathe in the fresh air.

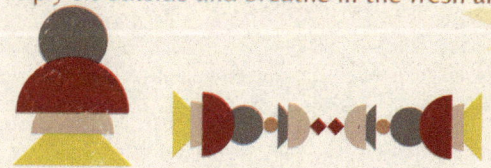

Self Care Examples

02

Practicing Gratitude:
Write down a few things you are grateful for each day. Focusing on the positives can improve your overall outlook on life.

Setting Boundaries:
Learn to say no when you need to. It is okay to set boundaries and protect your time and energy.

Talking to Someone You Trust:
Share your thoughts and feelings with a trusted friend, family member, or coach. Sometimes, talking things out can be incredibly helpful.

Self Care Plan

Goals For My Mind
What do I want to be thinking about the most?

1. _____
2. _____
3. _____
4. _____
5. _____

Goals For My Body
How do I want to move my body?

1. _____
2. _____
3. _____
4. _____
5. _____

Self Care Plan

Goals For My Emotions
How do I want to feel?

_____
_____
_____
_____
_____

Goals For My Spirit
What inspires me and brings me a sense of peace and purpose?

_____
_____
_____
_____
_____

What are SMART Goals?

SMART goals are a way to make sure your goals are clear and reachable. They help you focus on what you really want and figure out how to get there.

SMART goals help you stay on track and motivated, making it easier to achieve what you want!

Here's why they are important:
- Clarity: They make your goals clear and specific, so you know exactly what you are aiming for.
- Focus: They help you concentrate on what is important and avoid distractions.
- Motivation: Seeing your progress and knowing your goals are achievable keeps you motivated.
- Accountability: They make it easier to hold yourself accountable because you have a clear plan and deadline.
- Success: By breaking down big goals into smaller, manageable steps, SMART goals increase your chances of success.

Using SMART goals can turn your dreams into reality by giving you a solid plan to follow!

What are SMART Goals?

Here's what SMART stands for:
- Specific: Be clear about what you want to achieve. Instead of saying "I want to do better in school," say "I want to get an A in math."
- Measurable: Make sure you can track your progress. For example, "I will study math for 30 minutes every day" lets you see how much effort you're putting in.
- Achievable: Set a goal that you can actually reach. If you're getting a C in math now, aiming for an A is great, but a B might be a more achievable first step.
- Relevant: Choose a goal that really matters to you. If math is important for your future plans, then focusing on it makes sense.
- Time-bound: Give yourself a deadline. This way, you know when you want to achieve your goal by. For example, "I want to get an A in math by the end of the semester."

Goals

04

Make sure you follow the SMART structure when setting goals. Use the following questions to create your goals.
Are my goals.... specific? relevant? measurable? time based and achievable?

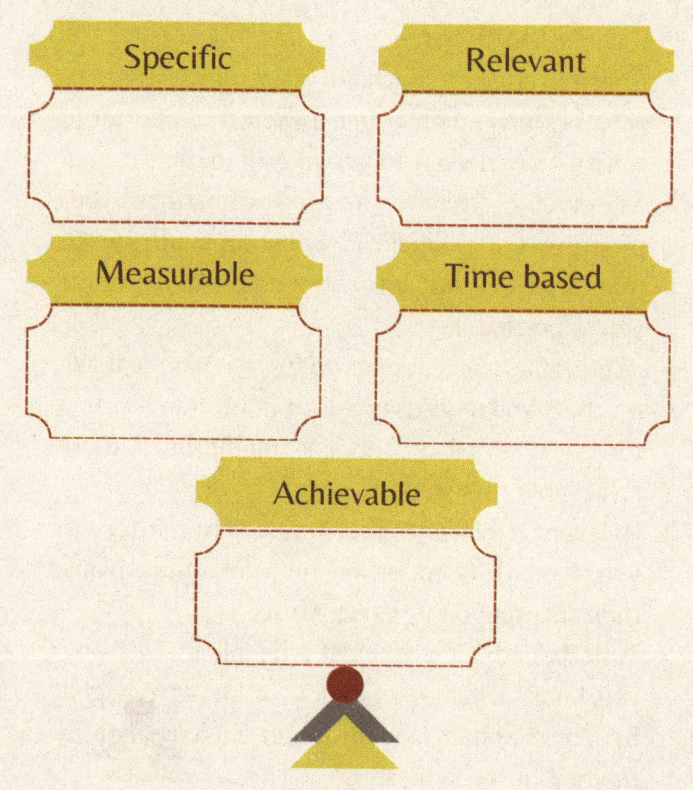

Specific

Relevant

Measurable

Time based

Achievable

Example

I will strengthen my relationship with my sibling by initiating a weekly game night where we play board games together for at least an hour.
I will do this every Friday evening for the next three months, starting this week.

This goal is specific, as it outlines the activity (playing board games) and the frequency (weekly).

It is measurable, as I can track my progress by noting each game night I successfully complete.

It is achievable, as I have the time and resources to organize a game night once a week.

It is relevant, as building a strong relationship with my sibling is important to me.

It is time-bound, as I have set a clear start date and end date for this goal (three months).

Mind Memo

_____
_____
_____
_____
_____

Use this space to express what it is in your mind

_____
_____
_____
_____
_____

Ideas

- Specific: "I will build empathy by volunteering at a local charity or community organization."

- Measurable: "I will keep a gratitude journal and write down three things I am thankful for every day."

- Achievable: "I will set aside time each week to have a meaningful conversation with a family member or friend."

- Relevant: "I will work on resolving conflicts peacefully by practicing active listening and compromising with others."

- Time-bound: "By the end of the semester, I will join a sports team or group activity to meet new people and make friends."

Ideas

- Specific: "I will initiate a conversation with a classmate I don't know well and ask them about their interests."
- Measurable: "I will make plans to hang out with a friend outside of school at least once a week."
- Achievable: "I will join a club or group related to my interests to meet new people and make friends."
- Relevant: "I will spend more quality time with my family by having dinner together at least three times a week."
- Time-bound: "By the end of the month, I will apologize to a friend for a past misunderstanding and work to rebuild our relationship."

- Specific: "I will improve my communication skills by practicing active listening during conversations with my friends and family."
- Measurable: "I will send a positive text message to a friend or family member every day to show appreciation for their support."
- Achievable: "I will work on controlling my temper by taking a deep breath and counting to ten before responding in a heated situation."
- Relevant: "I will learn more about my cultural background and traditions to better understand and connect with my family heritage."
- Time-bound: "Within the next month, I will plan a fun outing with my siblings to strengthen our bond."

Writing Down My SMART Goals

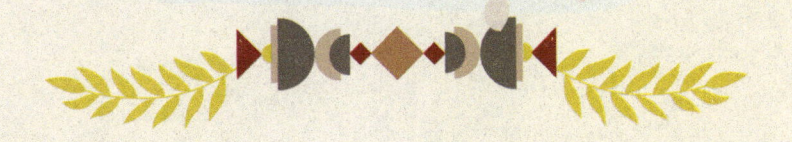

More SMART Goals

Thought Tracker

Gratitude

Gratitude is the practice of recognizing and appreciating the good things in life.

It is about acknowledging the positive experiences, people, and things that bring us joy and contentment.

Practising gratitude can have a profound impact on your mental and emotional well-being.

Let's explore why gratitude is important and how you can incorporate it into your daily life.

How Do I Express Gratitude?

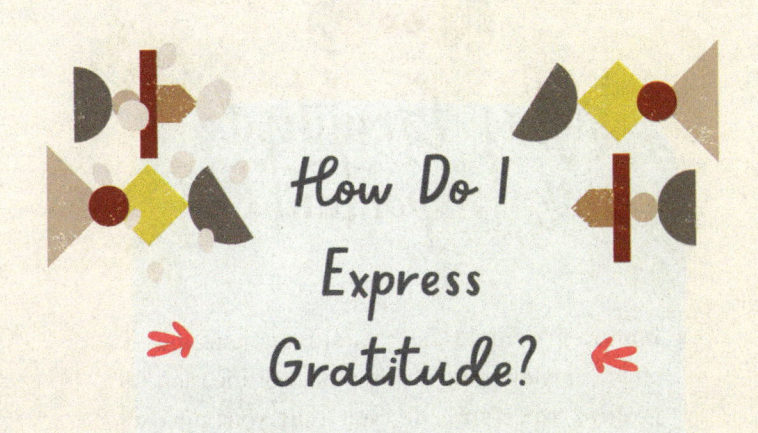

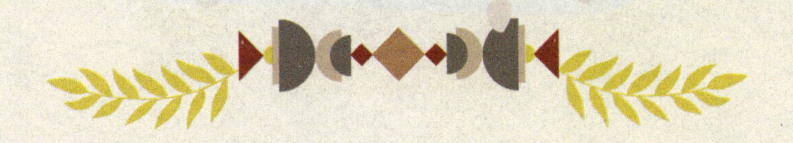

Why Gratitude is Important?

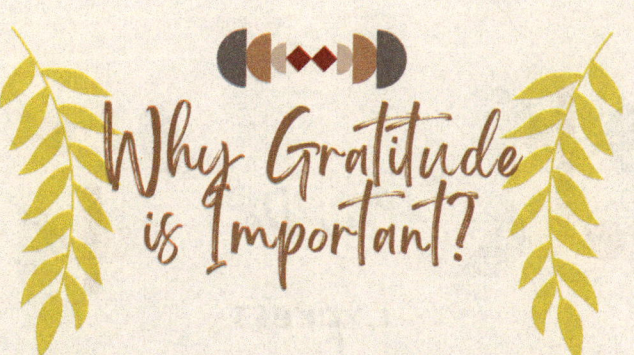

- **Improves Mental Health:** Gratitude helps reduce stress, anxiety, and depression. By focusing on positive aspects of life, you shift your mindset from negative thoughts to positive ones, which boosts your overall mood.

- **Enhances Relationships:** Expressing gratitude to others strengthens your relationships. When you show appreciation for the people in your life, it fosters a sense of connection and trust.

- **Boosts Self-Esteem:** Recognizing the good in your life and yourself can enhance your self-esteem. Gratitude helps you appreciate your strengths and achievements, making you feel more confident and valued.

Why Gratitude is Important?

- Increases Resilience: Grateful people are more resilient during tough times. By focusing on what they have rather than what they lack, they can navigate challenges with a positive outlook.

- Promotes a Positive Attitude: Regularly practicing gratitude cultivates a habit of looking for the good in every situation, leading to a more optimistic and positive attitude towards life.

Why is it important to ME to express Gratitude?

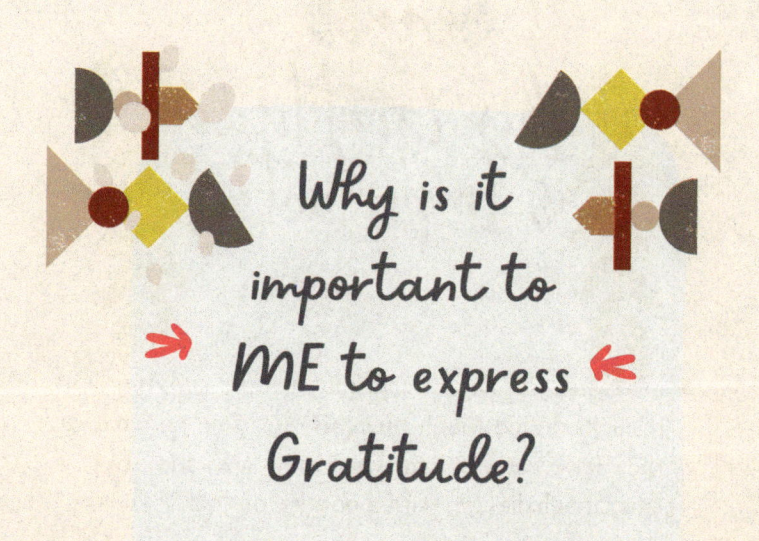

Gratitude List

I Am Grateful For...

How to Practice Gratitude

Gratitude Journal:
- What to Do: Keep a gratitude journal where you write down three things you're grateful for each day.

- How it Helps: This practice helps you focus on the positives in your life, even on challenging days. Over time, you'll start to notice more things to be thankful for.

Gratitude Letters:
- What to Do: Write a letter to someone you appreciate, explaining why you're grateful for them. You can choose to give it to them or keep it for yourself.

- How it Helps: Expressing gratitude directly to others can strengthen your relationships and make you feel more connected.

How to Practice Gratitude

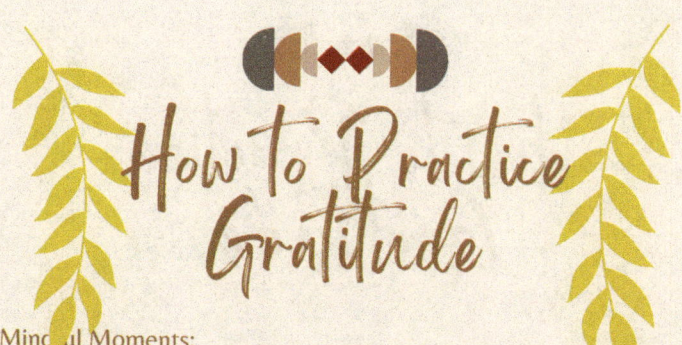

Mindful Moments:
- What to Do: Take a few moments each day to pause and reflect on the things you're thankful for. This can be done during your morning routine, before bed, or at any quiet time during the day.

- How it Helps: Mindful gratitude helps you stay present and aware of the good things in your life, fostering a sense of peace and contentment.

Gratitude Jar:
- What to Do: Use a jar to collect notes of gratitude. Each time something good happens or you feel thankful, write it down on a piece of paper and put it in the jar. At the end of the month or year, read through your notes.

- How it Helps: This visual representation of your gratitude can remind you of all the positive experiences you've had and lift your spirits when you're feeling down.

How to Practice Gratitude

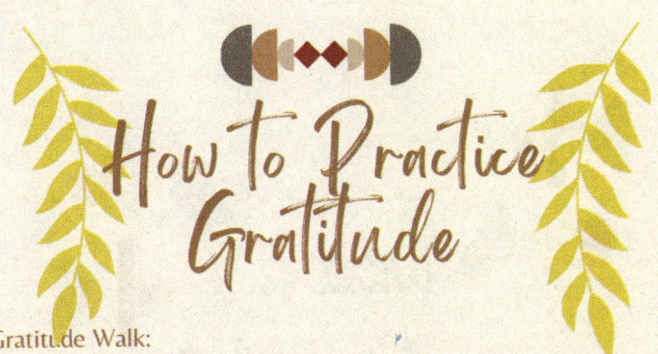

Gratitude Walk:
- What to Do: Take a walk outside and use the time to reflect on the things you are grateful for. Notice the beauty in nature, the kindness of people you encounter, or any positive experiences you've had.

- How it Helps: Combining physical activity with gratitude practice enhances your mood and helps you appreciate the world around you.

Gratitude Prompts:
- What to Do: Use prompts to guide your gratitude practice. Examples include:
    - What is something that made you smile today?
    - Who is someone who has helped you recently?

- How it Helps: Prompts can help you think of specific things to be grateful for and make your practice more focused and meaningful.

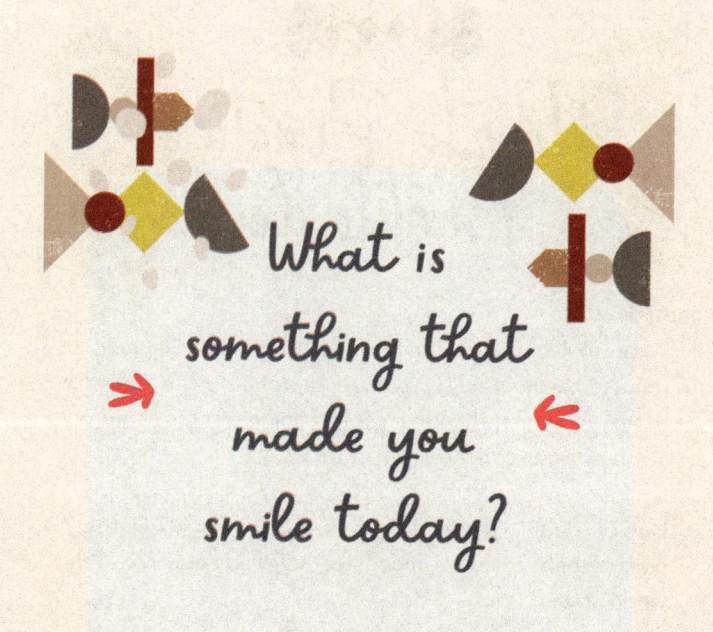

What is something that made you smile today?

Who is someone who has helped you recently?

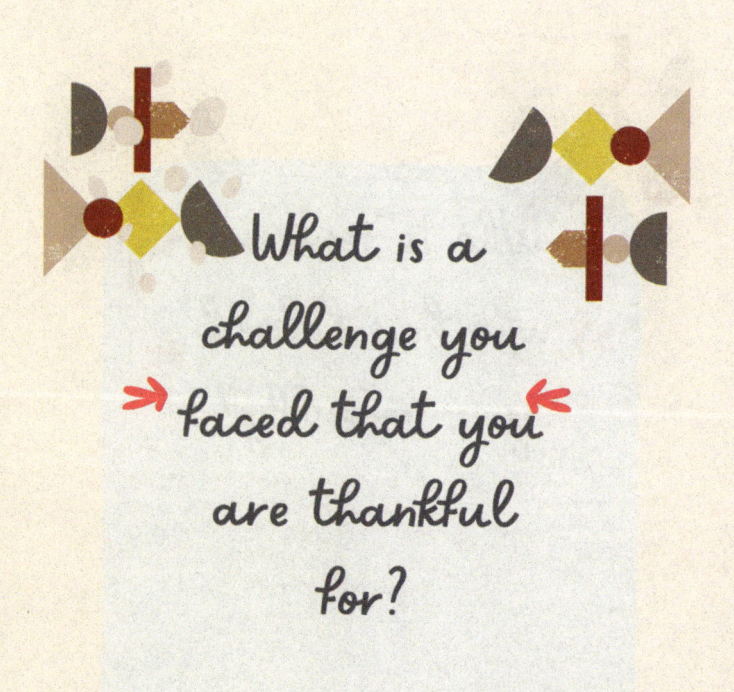

What is a challenge you faced that you are thankful for?

Kindness

Kindness is all about being friendly, generous, and considerate to others. It is about showing compassion and understanding, and making an effort to help and support the people around you.

Here is what kindness looks like:
- Being Friendly: Smiling at someone, saying hello, or starting a conversation can make someone's day better.
- Helping Others: Offering to help someone with their homework, carrying groceries, or simply listening to a friend who needs to talk.
- Showing Respect: Treating others the way you want to be treated, even if they are different from you.
- Being Supportive: Encouraging friends and family when they are going through a tough time or celebrating their achievements with them.
- Being Generous: Sharing what you have, whether it is your time, attention, or resources, with those who need it.

Kindness is important because it makes the world a better place. When you are kind to others, you not only make them feel good, but you also feel good about yourself. Plus, acts of kindness can inspire others to be kind too, creating a ripple effect of positivity. Remember, kindness doesn't have to be a big, grand gesture. Even small acts of kindness can have a huge impact!

What does Kindness mean to me?

_____
_____
_____
_____
_____
_____
_____
_____
_____
_____
_____
_____
_____
_____
_____

Where do I show kindness daily?

Thought Tracker

The Eisenhower Box

06

Simple yet powerful tool for prioritizing tasks and managing time effectively, this method helps you determine which tasks to focus on, delegate, or eliminate based on their urgency and importance.

	Urgent	Not Urgent
Important	Do	Decide
Not Important	Delegate	Delete

Fun Fact

This tool is named after President Dwight D. Eisenhower, who famously said, "What is important is seldom urgent, and what is urgent is seldom important."

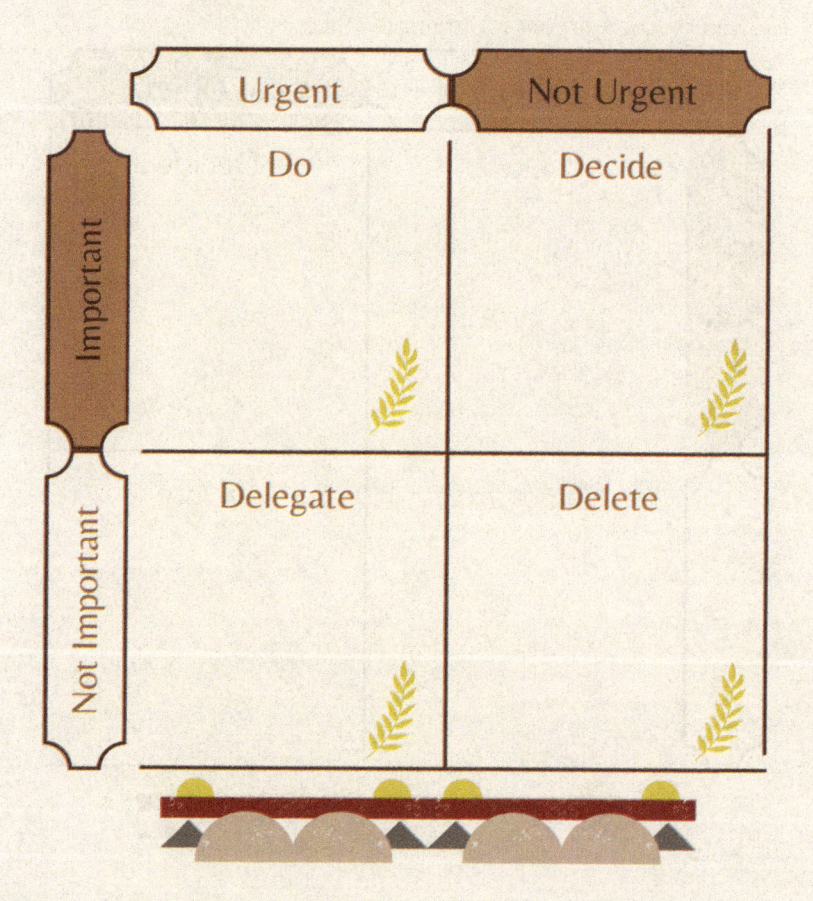

	Urgent	Not Urgent
Important	Do	Decide
Not Important	Delegate	Delete

➤ Use this space to list your tasks ⬅

Notes

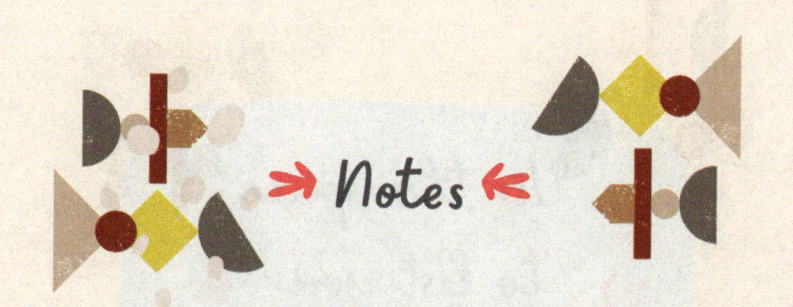

The box is divided into four quadrants

- Urgent and Important (Do)

Tasks that are both urgent and important should be done immediately. These are tasks that require your immediate attention and contribute directly to your goals or well-being.

Examples: studying for an upcoming exam, completing a homework assignment due the next day, or responding to a time-sensitive message from a friend.

- Important, but Not Urgent (Schedule)

Tasks that are important but not urgent should be scheduled for later. These are tasks that contribute to your long-term goals or well-being but do not require immediate action.

Examples planning a study schedule for the semester, researching colleges or career options, or starting a personal project or hobby.

The box is divided into four quadrants

- Urgent, but Not Important (Delegate)

Tasks that are urgent but not important should be delegated if possible. These are tasks that require immediate action but do not contribute significantly to your goals or well-being.

Examples running an errand for a family member, helping a friend with a non-urgent task, or attending to a minor school-related issue.

- Not Urgent and Not Important (Eliminate)

Tasks that are neither urgent nor important should be eliminated. These are tasks that do not contribute to your goals or well-being and can be considered a waste of time.

Examples spending excessive time on social media, watching TV shows or playing video games excessively, or engaging in gossip or drama.

Mind Memo

_____
_____
_____
_____
_____

Use this space to express what it is in your mind

_____
_____
_____
_____
_____

How to Use It Effectively

- **Identify Tasks:** Start by listing all your tasks and categorizing them into the four quadrants based on their urgency and importance.

- **Prioritize:** Focus on completing tasks in the "Do" quadrant first, as these are both urgent and important. Then, move on to tasks in the "Schedule" quadrant, followed by tasks in the "Delegate" quadrant.

- **Schedule Regular Review:** Regularly review your tasks and update the Eisenhower Box as needed. Some tasks may change in urgency or importance over time.

- **Avoid Procrastination:** By using the Eisenhower Box, you can avoid procrastinating on important tasks and ensure you are focusing your time and energy on activities that truly matter to you.

- **Achieve Balance:** The Eisenhower Box helps you achieve a balance between addressing immediate needs and working towards your long-term goals, promoting a sense of accomplishment and well-being.

Notes

Notes

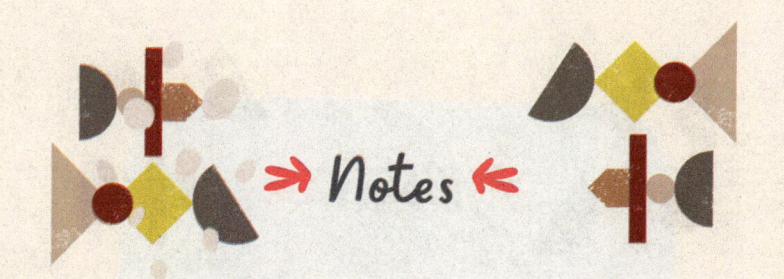

Thought Tracker

Eating Right

Self-care

Eating right is a fundamental aspect of self-care that has a profound impact on both your physical and mental well-being. As a teen, your body is growing and changing rapidly, and the food you eat plays a crucial role in supporting that growth, giving you energy, and helping you feel your best.

Favorite Foods	Favorite Drinks

Why Eating Right Matters

1. Energy and Vitality:
    - Eating a balanced diet gives you the energy you need to stay active and alert throughout the day. Foods rich in nutrients help fuel your body and keep you feeling energetic.
2. Growth and Development:
    - During your teen years, your body undergoes significant changes. Nutrients such as protein, calcium, iron, and vitamins are essential for proper growth, bone health, and muscle development.
3. Mental Health:
    - The food you eat can affect your mood and mental health. A diet rich in fruits, vegetables, whole grains, and lean proteins can help improve your mood, reduce stress, and enhance your cognitive function.
4. Long-Term Health:
    - Developing healthy eating habits now can set the foundation for a lifetime of good health. Eating right helps prevent chronic diseases like obesity, diabetes, and heart disease.

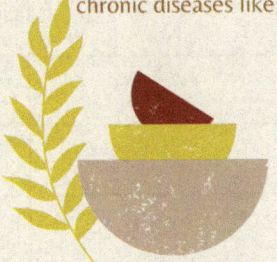

Mind Memo

Use this space to express what it is in your mind

Tips for Eating Healthy

1. **Eat a Balanced Diet:**
   - Include a variety of foods in your diet to ensure you get all the essential nutrients. Your meals should include fruits, vegetables, whole grains, lean proteins, and healthy fats.
2. **Stay Hydrated:**
   - Drink plenty of water throughout the day. Staying hydrated is important for your overall health, including your energy levels and concentration.
3. **Limit Processed Foods:**
   - Try to minimize your intake of processed foods, sugary snacks, and drinks. These foods often contain empty calories, unhealthy fats, and high levels of sugar and salt.
4. **Healthy Snacking:**
   - Choose healthy snacks like fruits, nuts, yogurt, or whole-grain crackers instead of chips, candy, or sugary treats. Healthy snacks can help you maintain your energy levels and keep hunger at bay.
5. **Listen to Your Body:**
   - Pay attention to your hunger and fullness cues. Eat when you're hungry and stop when you're full. Avoid eating out of boredom or stress.
6. **Plan Your Meals:**
   - Planning your meals ahead of time can help you make healthier choices and avoid last-minute junk food. Try to include a mix of different food groups in each meal.
7. **Enjoy Your Food:**
   - Take the time to enjoy your meals without distractions. Eating mindfully helps you appreciate your food and recognize when you're full.

Research about your favourite foods, found out how much they nurture you & summarise it here

Thought Tracker

Meal Planner

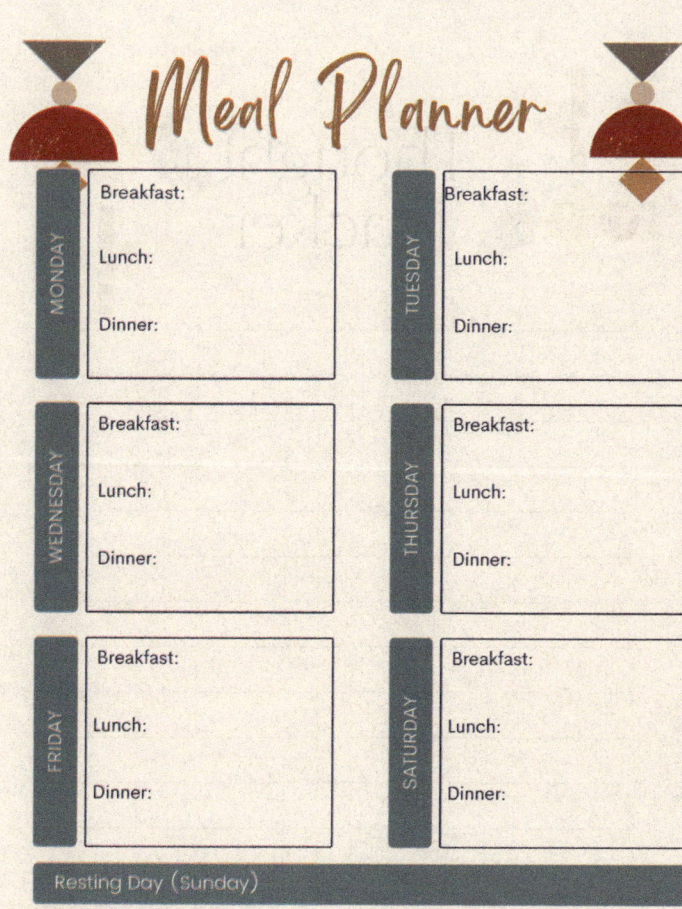

MONDAY
Breakfast:

Lunch:

Dinner:

TUESDAY
Breakfast:

Lunch:

Dinner:

WEDNESDAY
Breakfast:

Lunch:

Dinner:

THURSDAY
Breakfast:

Lunch:

Dinner:

FRIDAY
Breakfast:

Lunch:

Dinner:

SATURDAY
Breakfast:

Lunch:

Dinner:

Resting Day (Sunday)
Breakfast:

Lunch:

Dinner:

Snack:

Notes

Mind Memo

Use this space to express what it is in your mind

Simple Meal Ideas

Breakfast:
Whole-grain toast with avocado and a boiled egg
Greek yogurt with berries and a sprinkle of granola
A smoothie made with spinach, banana, and almond milk

Lunch:
A salad with mixed greens, grilled chicken, cherry tomatoes, and a light vinaigrette
A whole-grain wrap with turkey, lettuce, tomato, and hummus
Quinoa bowl with black beans, corn, bell peppers, and a squeeze of lime

Dinner:
Grilled salmon with a side of steamed broccoli and brown rice
Stir-fried tofu with mixed vegetables and whole-grain noodles
Baked chicken breast with sweet potato and a side of green beans

Snacks:
Apple slices with peanut butter
Carrot sticks with hummus
A handful of almonds and a piece of dark chocolate

List all you ate yesterday

Notes

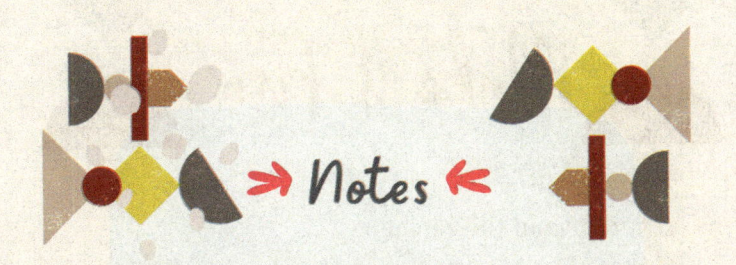

Awareness is crucial when it comes to food because it helps you make healthier choices and build a positive relationship with eating. Here are a few reasons why being aware of your food and eating habits is important

Make it Fun

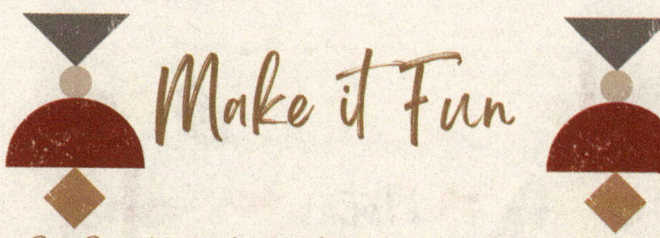

Get Creative in the Kitchen:
- Experiment with new recipes and ingredients. Cooking can be a fun and rewarding way to take care of yourself.

Involve Friends and Family:
- Share meals with friends and family. Cooking and eating together can be a great way to bond and enjoy healthy food.

Learn About Nutrition:
- Take some time to learn about the benefits of different foods and how they impact your health. Understanding nutrition can empower you to make better choices.

Food Tracker

Food Tracker

Exercise
Self-care

08

Exercise is a powerful form of self-care that supports your overall health and well-being. By making physical activity a regular part of your routine, you're investing in yourself and setting the stage for a healthy, active lifestyle. Find what you love, set goals, and enjoy the journey to a stronger, happier you!

Types of Exercise
Aerobic (Cardio)
   Activities that get your heart pumping and improve cardiovascular health, such as running, cycling, swimming, and dancing.
Strength Training:
   Exercises that build muscle strength and endurance, like weightlifting, resistance band workouts, and bodyweight exercises (e.g., push-ups, squats).
Flexibility and Balance:
   Activities that improve flexibility, balance, and coordination, such as yoga, Pilates, and stretching exercises.
Sports and Recreational Activities:
   Engaging in sports like soccer, basketball, tennis, or any recreational activity that you enjoy and keeps you moving.

My Favorite Exercises
1.
2.
3.
4.
5.
6.
7.
8.
9.
10.

Mind Memo

Use this space to express what it is in your mind

Why Exercise Matters

Physical Health:
- Strength and Endurance: Regular exercise helps build and maintain strong muscles and bones. Activities like weight training, running, and sports can improve your strength and endurance.
- Heart Health: Cardiovascular exercises, such as swimming, biking, and jogging, improve heart and lung function, reducing the risk of heart disease.
- Weight Management: Exercise helps regulate your weight by burning calories and increasing your metabolism. It also supports healthy growth and development.

Mental Health:
- Stress Relief: Physical activity releases endorphins, which are natural mood lifters that help reduce stress and anxiety.
- Improved Mood: Regular exercise can boost your self-esteem and overall sense of well-being. It can help combat feelings of depression and improve your outlook on life.
- Better Sleep: Engaging in physical activity can help you fall asleep faster and enjoy deeper, more restful sleep.

Why Exercise Matters

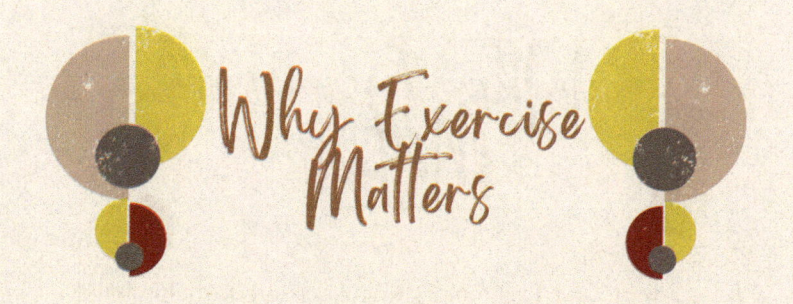

Cognitive Benefits:
- Enhanced Focus: Exercise increases blood flow to the brain, which can improve concentration and cognitive function.
- Memory Improvement: Physical activity has been shown to enhance memory and learning capabilities.

Social Benefits:
- Teamwork and Social Skills: Participating in team sports or group activities helps you develop social skills, teamwork, and cooperation.
- Building Friendships: Exercise can be a great way to meet new people and build lasting friendships.

List favorite types of exercises

How can I make exercise fun?

List of friends I would like to exercise with

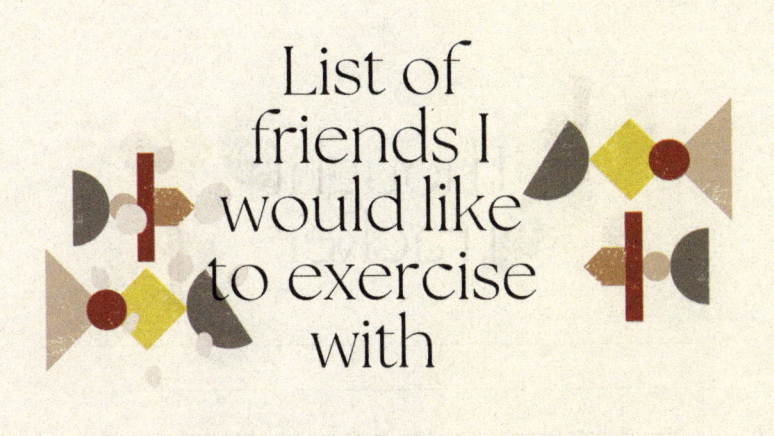

Thought Tracker

Building Relationships
Self-care

09

Building and nurturing healthy relationships is a vital part of self-care that enhances your emotional well-being and happiness.

By investing time and effort into your relationships, you create a supportive and loving network that enriches your life.

Be a good listener, show appreciation, be honest, and spend quality time with the people you care about.

These actions will help you build strong, meaningful connections that provide joy, support, and a sense of belonging throughout your teen years and beyond.

Building Relationships
Self-care

Healthy relationships provide support, understanding, and a sense of belonging.

My Closest People

1.
2.
3.
4.
5.
6.
7.
8.
9.
10.

Building Relationships
Reflection

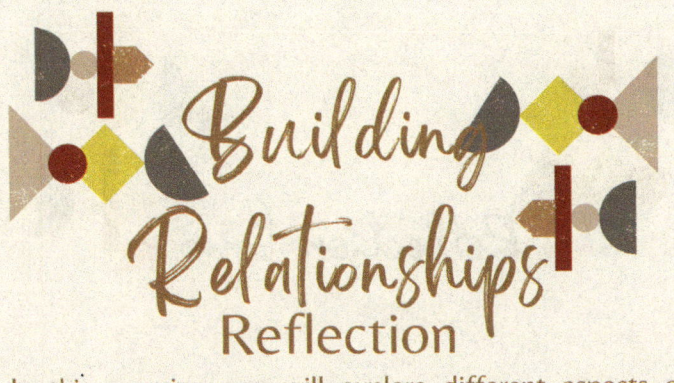

In this exercise, you will explore different aspects of building relationships and learn practical strategies for nurturing them.

Take a few moments to reflect on the following questions:

1. What does a healthy relationship look like to you?
2. Why are relationships important for your well-being?
3. What challenges do you face in building and maintaining relationships?
4. What qualities do you value in a friend or family member?

Reflection time

Notes

Thought Tracker

Thought Tracker

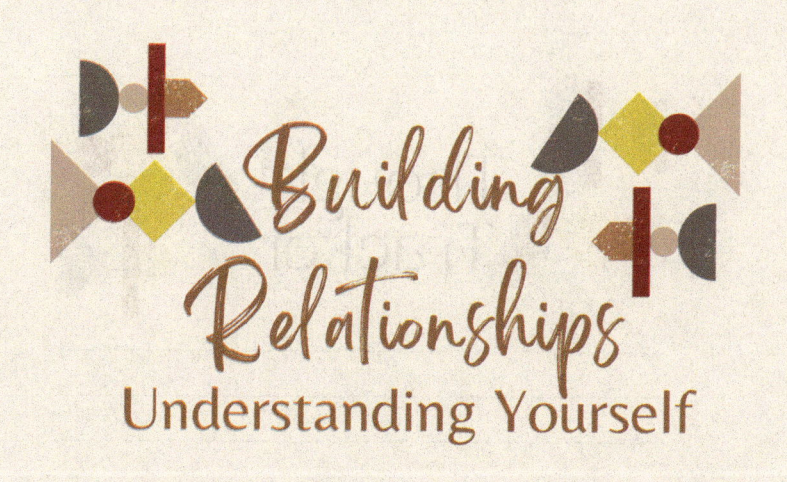

Building Relationships
Understanding Yourself

1. Identify Your Values: List three values that are important to you in a relationship (e.g., trust, honesty, respect).
2. Recognize Your Strengths: Write down three qualities or skills that you bring to a relationship (e.g., good listener, sense of humor, empathy).
3. Set Boundaries: Think about your personal boundaries in relationships. Write down one boundary you want to set or maintain in your relationships.

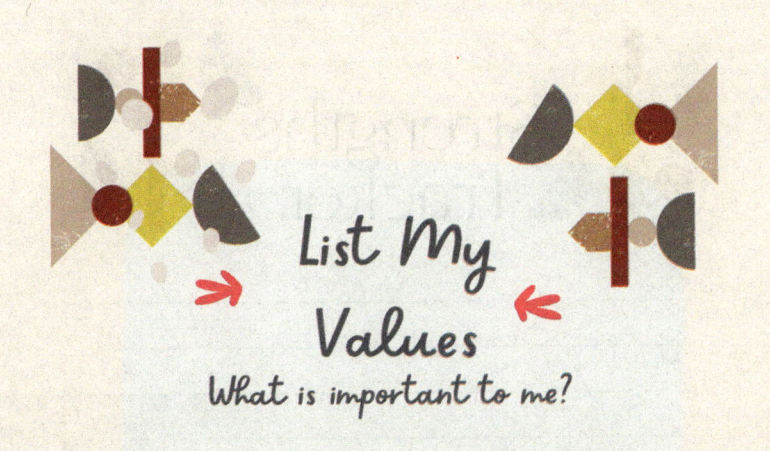

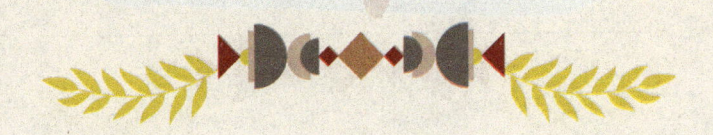

List My Values
What is important to me?

Strengths Tracker

List My Boundaries

Building Relationships

Building Healthy Relationships

1. **Effective Communication:** Practice active listening skills by having a conversation with a friend or family member. Focus on listening without interrupting and responding with empathy.
2. **Empathy and Understanding:** Put yourself in someone else's shoes. Think about a situation from their perspective and write down how you think they might feel.
3. **Conflict Resolution:** Think about a recent disagreement you had with someone. Write down how you could have handled the situation differently to resolve the conflict peacefully.
4. **Quality Time:** Plan a fun activity with a friend or family member. Focus on enjoying each other's company and strengthening your bond.
5. **Gratitude and Appreciation:** Write a thank-you note to someone who has been supportive or kind to you. Express your appreciation for their presence in your life.

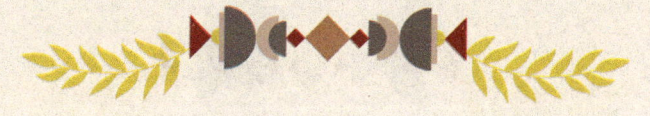

Mind Memo

_____
_____
_____
_____
_____

Use this space to express what it is in your mind

_____
_____
_____
_____
_____

Mind Memo

Use this space to express what it is in your mind

Building Relationships
Action Plan

Set Goals: Write down one relationship goal you want to achieve (e.g., improve communication with a family member, make a new friend).

Action Steps: List three action steps you can take to work towards your goal (e.g., initiate a conversation, join a club or group, attend a social event).

Timeline: Set a timeline for achieving your goal. Break down your action steps into manageable tasks and assign deadlines to each.

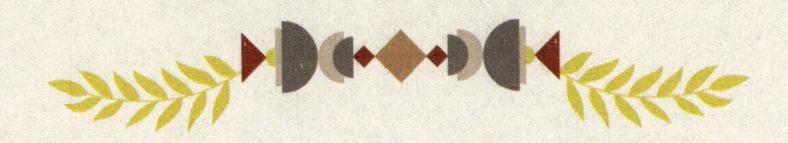

Set Relationships Goals

… Action Steps …

Timeline for achieving my goals

_____
_____
_____
_____
_____
_____
_____
_____
_____
_____
_____
_____
_____
_____
_____

Thought Tracker

Thought Tracker

Congratulations!

You have reached the end of your Mindful Moments Adventure workbook, and what an incredible journey it has been!

Every page you filled, every thought you tracked, and every moment you reflected on has brought you one step closer to understanding yourself and building stronger, healthier relationships.

But remember, this is just the beginning. The insights and habits you have developed are powerful tools that will continue to guide you through life's ups and downs. Keep exploring, keep reflecting, and keep growing.

Your journey of self-discovery and relationship-building is a lifelong adventure, and you are equipped with the skills and mindset to make it a fulfilling and joyful one.

Your Next Steps

- **Keep Writing:** Even though this workbook is complete, don't stop capturing your thoughts and experiences. Start a new notebook, digital document, or even continue on blank pages here. Your future self will thank you for it!

- **Practice Mindfulness:** Make mindfulness a daily habit. Whether it's through meditation, journaling, or simply taking a few moments to breathe and center yourself, these practices will help you stay grounded and present.

- **Nurture Relationships:** Keep building and maintaining healthy relationships. Use the skills you've learned to communicate effectively, show empathy, and support those around you.

- **Set New Goals:** Continuously set new SMART goals for yourself. Personal growth is a never-ending journey, and having clear, achievable goals will keep you motivated and focused.

Keep Writing

Write an encouraging message for yourself

Stay Connected

I would love to hear about your journey and how this Mindful Moments Workbook has helped you.
Stay connected and share your experiences, questions, or even just a friendly hello.

Here is how you can reach me:

Email: info@lucianapierangeli.com
Instagram: lucianapierangeli8
Website: www.lucianapierangeli.com
LinkedIn: www.linkedin.com/in/lucianapierangeli/

Thank You!

Thank you for allowing me to be a part of your journey.

Remember, you are capable of achieving amazing things, and I am here to support you every step of the way.

Keep shining, keep growing, and keep being the incredible person you are.

Until Next Time...

Stay curious, stay inspired, and never stop exploring the wonders of your mind and the world around you.

Keep your vibe high!

With Love

Luciana

Made in the USA
Columbia, SC
14 February 2025